Augsburg College
George Sverdrup Library
Minneapolis, Minnesota 55404

Series / Number 03-012

Determinants of Public Policy in the American States: A Model for Synthesis

YONG HYO CHO
The University of Akron

H. GEORGE FREDERICKSON
Indiana University

SAGE PUBLICATIONS / Beverly Hills / London

Copyright © 1973 by Sage Publications, Inc.

Printed in the United States of America

All rights reserved. No part of this book may be reproduced or utilized in any form or by any means, electronic or mechanical, including photocopying, recording, or by any information storage and retrieval system, without permission in writing from the publisher.

For information address:

SAGE PUBLICATIONS, INC.
275 South Beverly Drive
Beverly Hills, California 90212

SAGE PUBLICATIONS LTD
St George's House / 44 Hatton Garden
London EC1N 8ER

International Standard Book Number 0-8039-0299-9

Library of Congress Catalog Card No. 73-84165

FIRST PRINTING

When citing a professional paper, please use the proper form. Remember to cite the correct Sage Professional Paper series title and include the paper number. One of the two following formats can be adapted (depending on the style manual used):

(1) OSTROM, E. et al. (1973) "Community Organization and the Provision of Police Services." Sage Professional Papers in Administrative and Policy Studies, 1, 03-001. Beverly Hills and London: Sage Pubns.

OR

(2) Ostrom, Elinor, et al. 1973. *Community Organization and the Provision of Police Services.* Sage Professional Papers in Administrative and Policy Studies, vol. 1, series no. 03-001. Beverly Hills and London: Sage Publications.

CONTENTS

Chapter I. Introduction 5

Chapter II. Research Design 8
    Policy Measures (Dependent Variables) 8
    Policy Determinants (Independent Variables) 11
    Analytical Technique 13

Chapter III. Findings 14
    The 1962 Results 15
    The 1967-1969 Results 24

Chapter IV. Influence Typology of Policy Determinants 34
    Synthesis 34
    The Scope of Influence 35
    The Intensity of Influence 39
    Typology of Influence 43

Chapter V. Conclusion 47

Notes 52

References 55

YONG HYO CHO is a professor of Political Science and Urban Studies and Associate Director of the Center for Urban Studies at the University of Akron. He received his M.P.A. and Ph.D. from Syracuse University. He has authored numerous articles, book chapters and monographs on the subject of politics and public policy of state and city governments. He has just completed a book manuscript on Public Policy and Urban Crime.

H. GEORGE FREDERICKSON is Associate Dean for Policy and Administrative Studies of the School of Public and Environmental Affairs, Indiana University. He has served as associate director, Metropolitan Studies Program, Maxwell Graduate School, Syracuse University; and, as Fellow in Higher Education, University of North Carolina. He is the author of numerous articles in the field of public administration, especially in the area of organization theory. His publications include Neighborhood Control in the 70's and Power, Opinion and Policy in Syracuse (with Linda Schluter O'Leary). He is currently working on a forthcoming study of public administration from a theoretical perspective. Dr. Frederickson is a member of the executive committee of the national council, American Society for Public Administration, and also serves as research editor, PUBLIC ADMINISTRATION REVIEW.

Determinants of Public Policy in the American States: A Model for Synthesis

YONG HYO CHO
The University of Akron

H. GEORGE FREDERICKSON
Indiana University

CHAPTER I
INTRODUCTION

What are the important forces affecting policy variation among the American states? This question has been the subject of systematic research for nearly two decades. As a consequence, we are better informed about the relationships of socioeconomic and political-governmental variables and the patterns of policy variation.

However, the research results are not without confusion from the standpoint of attempting systematic generalizations as to the patterns of determinant influence on policy decisions. The reasons for confusion are complex, but we shall focus on the following two: (1) The research results are confusing and in some cases in conflict. Most of the earlier studies conclude that economic conditions are the primary determinants of policy outcomes, while more recent studies confont this conclusion with evidence of salience of political-governmental influence; and (2) From a methodo-

---

AUTHORS' NOTE: *This study is a part of the Reapportionment Project of the Metropolitan Studies Program, the Maxwell Graduate School of Citizenship and Public Affairs, Syracuse University. The project was supported by the National Municipal League. We especially appreciate the roles played by Alan K. Campbell, Guthrie Birkhead, William Cassella, and William Boyd in the development of our research. Several persons contributed to the research effort, most notably Robert Firestine, Jack Rossotti, and John Bacheller. We alone are responsible for the results.*
Y.H.C.
H.G.F.

logical perspective, the scope and context of policy analyses seem to contribute to the confusing results. Nearly without exception, the scope of each piece of research is narrowly defined and its context of inquiry is too particularistic to permit generalizations. Policy variables are usually homogeneous and independent variables fail to represent diverse indicators of political-governmental characteristics. Often a political or governmental variable is included in the analysis to test a specific point of particular interest at the expense of general implications of policy determinants.

The main purpose of this study is to indicate that there are identifiable patterns of influence relationships between socioeconomic and political-governmental variables and measures of public policy outcomes in the states. To achieve this purpose, we have made special efforts to broaden the scope of analysis and context of inquiry. We include a broad range of policy variables and socioeconomic and political-governmental variables in our analysis. We adopt a longitudinal approach to cover two points of time rather than one in our analysis. We address ourselves to some general, exploratory propositions rather than to specific hypotheses of particularistic importance.

A brief review of literature will make it clear why this undertaking is necessary. Solomon Fabricant (1952), an economist and pioneer in the comparative analysis of state fiscal behavior, found economic affluence and urbanism the central force in accounting for the variation of per capita state and local expenditures. Among political scientists, V. O. Key, Jr. (1949) hypothesized the potential significance of party competition for the explanation of state welfare policy variance in the late 1940s.

A large number of studies in the 1960s by economists and political scientists (Fisher, 1964; Dye, 1966; Dawson and Robinson, 1963) were devoted to this subject . In most instances, the research findings concluded that the policy variance among the states is primarily the result of the difference in economic development rather than difference in political conditions or political-governmental systems. Recently, however, several studies have found evidence that political and governmental variables are important determinants of policy variance.

Charles F. Cnudde and Donald J. McCrone (1969) concluded that political party competition does have a significant impact on some welfare policies (the primary example being aid to dependent children) though such influence is not evident in all welfare policy areas. Brian Fry and Richard Winters (1970) found that political variables in aggregate are more powerful in accounting for the "redistributive" fiscal policy of the states than are social and economic variables. Alan Pulsipher and James Weatherby (1968) tested the effect of political party competition and legislative apportionment for state and local expenditure variance. They found both party competition and apportionment to be statistically significant predictors for some important expenditure functions. More recently, our study (1973) of legislative apportionment and state fiscal policy proved that apportionment is a significant variable in accounting for the variance of many of the states' spending and taxing policies.

Seymore Sacks and Robert Harris (1964) found that the combined influence of population density, urbanization, and per capita income on state and local government expenditures for all functions and for selected functions declined rather sharply from 1942 to 1957 and 1960. Richard I. Hofferbert (1966) also discovered that per capita personal income and urbanization are more highly correlated with state fiscal policy variables in 1940 than in 1963. The trends discerned by Sacks and Harris, and Hofferbert suggest that political-governmental influences on policy outcomes may be growing through time.

These developments suggest the need for a comprehensive re-examination of the influence relationships of socioeconomic and political-governmental variables to policy variance among the states. Neither economic determinism nor the fragmented evidence of the salience of political influence seems to fully approximate the complex reality of state policy-making process. Nevertheless, an evaluation of the weak spots of the earlier studies serves as a point of departure in constructing our approach for re-examination.

First, we recognize that the discipline of political science has only recently begun the systematic study of policy process and its consequences. Presently available variables, particularly political and governmental variables, are at best crude. Yet the policy implications of the available political and governmental variables are not fully explored in a single study. Second, policy measures employed in earlier studies were generally one dimensional, each piece of research considered more or less homogeneous, such as expenditure or tax levels. Third, previous research suffers from a notable lack of concern for the "unit of analysis" problem. Most analysts mixed state and local jurisdictions as a unit of analysis for interstate comparison. We do recognize that the degree of interdependency between state and local governments is intimate in fiscal affairs as well as other governmental processes, but state government is a distinct decision-making unit separate from political subdivisions at the local level.[1]

As our exploratory guides, we submit the following propositions.

First, we posit three possibilities of influence relationships of socioeconomic and political-governmental variables to public policy decisions; socioeconomic dominant, political-governmental dominant, and socioeconomic and political-governmental shared control. Our reasoning for this proposition is this. State policies are distinct in their decision-making substance and context, effected in varying ways and magnitude by socioeconomic or political-governmental variables. The dominance of particular influences is seldom alike in their relevancy to all policy decisions.

Second, we posit the possibility of discernible influence types of socioeconomic or political-governmental variables in relation to a broad range of policy variables. It may be that some economic or political variables affect a broad range of policy areas and their effect is strong, while others affect a narrow range of policy areas and their influence is weak. Further, this influence type may be consistent from policy period to policy period for some variables and inconsistent for other variables.

Third, we posit that political-governmental influence gains strength through time. Our reasoning for this proposition is based on two separate pieces of evidence. Earlier research findings indicate that policy influence of socioeconomic variables tends to decline over time, therefore, we assume that political-governmental influence is increasing. Socioeconomic conditions among the states generally tend toward equalization while policy outcomes continue to vary widely. Thus, our prediction is that political-governmental differences are likely to account for more policy variation.

To explore these propositions and to attempt to overcome the weaknesses of previous research we (1) approach our analysis temporally, (2) use the most sophisticated available variables, and (3) solve the unit of analysis problem. Our model for analysis explains how this is done.

CHAPTER II
RESEARCH DESIGN

This paper reports the results of part of a larger research project aimed at assessing the impact of legislative apportionment on state policy outcomes. Therefore, the variables used for the measurement of public policy outcomes as well as those for socioeconomic, and political-governmental indicators are derived from the data bank created for the parental study.

POLICY MEASURES (DEPENDENT VARIABLES)

We selected state fiscal measures as our policy or dependent variables because they are easier to measure and to compare. We recognize that fiscal policies represent only a part of state policy decisions though they are important policy areas. We attempted to select as many types of fiscal measures as possible so as to provide a variety of meaningful policy types so as to satisfy our analytical needs. Fiscal policy variables so selected represent six categories and number 92 in total as follows:

(1) levels of per capita state spending.
(2) rates of change in the levels of per capita state spending.
(3) differentials in per capita state aid to metropolitan versus non-metropolitan areas.
(4) levels of per capita state taxation.
(5) rates of change in the levels of per capita state taxes.
(6) redistributive patterns of state fiscal policy for lower income groups.

The specific dependent variables used within each of these categories are listed below:

(1) Levels of Per Capita Spending.
   A. Total general expenditures, 1962 and 1969.
   B. Total direct expenditures, 1962 and 1969.
   C. General expenditures for education, 1962 and 1969.
   D. Direct expenditures for education, 1962 and 1969.
   E. Expenditures for institutions of higher education, 1962 and 1969.
   F. General expenditures for highways, 1962 and 1969.
   G. Direct expenditures for highways, 1962 and 1969.
   H. General expenditures for public welfare, 1962 and 1969.
   I. General expenditures for health and hospitals, 1962 and 1969.
   J. General expenditures for hospitals, 1962 and 1969.
   K. General expenditures for health, 1962 and 1969.
   L. General expenditures for natural resources, 1962 and 1969.
   M. General expenditures for correction, 1962 and 1969.
   N. Total intergovernmental expenditures, 1962 and 1969.
   O. Intergovernmental expenditures for education, 1962 and 1969.
   P. Intergovernmental expenditures for highways, 1962 and 1969.

(2) Rates of Change in the Levels of Per Capita State Spending.
   A. Percent change in total general expenditures, from 1957 to 1962 and from 1962 to 1969.
   B. Percent change in total direct expenditures, from 1957 to 1962 and from 1962 to 1969.
   C. Percent change in general expenditures for education, from 1957 to 1962 and from 1962 to 1969.

D. Percent change in direct expenditure for education, from 1957 to 1962 and from 1962 to 1969.
E. Percent change in expenditure for institutions of higher education, from 1957 to 1962 and from 1962 to 1969.
F. Percent change in general expenditures for highways, from 1957 to 1962 and from 1962 to 1969.
G. Percent change in general expenditures for public welfare, from 1957 to 1962 and from 1962 to 1969.
H. Percent change in general expenditures for health and hospitals, from 1957 to 1962 and from 1962 to 1969.
I. Percent change in general expenditures for natural resources, from 1957 to 1962 and from 1962 to 1969.
J. Percent change in total intergovernmental expenditures, from 1957 to 1962 and from 1962 to 1969.
K. Percent change in intergovernmental expenditures for education, from 1957 to 1962 and from 1962 to 1969.
L. Percent change in intergovernmental expenditures for highways, from 1957 to 1962 and from 1962 to 1969.

(3) Differentials in Per Capita State Aid to Metropolitan Versus Non-Metropolitan Areas.
A. Total state aid to non-metropolitan areas as a percent of that to metropolitan areas, 1962 and 1967.
B. Per pupil state aid to non-metropolitan areas as a percent of that to metropolitan areas, 1962 and 1967.
C. Per capita state and local expenditures for public welfare in non-metropolitan areas as a percent of that in metropolitan areas, 1962 and 1967.[2]
D. State direct expenditure for public welfare in non-metropolitan areas as a percent of that in metropolitan areas, 1962 and 1967.
E. Per capita state direct expenditure for highways in non-metropolitan areas as a percent of that in metropolitan areas, 1962 and 1967.
F. Percent of road mileage under state control in non-metropolitan areas as a percent of that in metropolitan areas, 1962 and 1967.

(4) Redistributive Patterns of State Fiscal Policy for Lower Income Groups.
A. The ratio of the benefits of state spending to state tax burdens for low income groups, 1961.[3]
B. The ratio of state and local expenditure benefits to state and local tax burdens, 1967.[4]

(5) Levels of Per Capita State Taxation:
A. Total taxes, 1962 and 1969.
B. Total sales taxes, 1962 and 1969.
C. Personal income taxes, 1962.
D. Corporation income taxes, 1962.
E. Property taxes, 1962.

(6) Rates of Change in Levels of Per Capita State Taxes:
   A. Percent of change in total taxes, from 1957 to 1962 and from 1962 to 1969.
   B. Percent change in sales taxes, from 1957 to 1962 and from 1962 to 1969.
   C. Percent change in personal income taxes, from 1957 to 1962.
   D. Percent change in corporate income taxes, from 1957 to 1962.
   E. Percent change in property taxes, from 1957 to 1962.

POLICY DETERMINANTS (INDEPENDENT VARIABLES)

Sixty-seven socioeconomic, and political-governmental indicators are selected to evaluate their relationships to the variance of the 92 state fiscal policy measures just described. Except several of the apportionment measures that we developed (which include Gini, Incumbency Success Ratio, Time-Lapse, and Session-Lapse) all the other political-governmental variables are adopted from appropriate literature. Socioeconomic variables are all derived from various U.S. Bureau of the Census publications. The only exception to this is the measure for inequality of income distribution, which is adopted from Dye (1969a).

These 67 economic and political indicators are classified into six political-governmental categories and two socioeconomic categories based on our judgment of their compatibility conceptually and functionally. The six political-governmental categories are legislative apportionment, political party systems, political participation, governmental modernism, state fiscal systems, and political conflict.[5] The two socioeconomic categories include economic development and urbanism.

The specific independent variables used are listed under appropriate categories below:

A. Apportionment

1962 Measures of Malapportionment
1. Schubert-Press
2. ICV
3. David-Eisenburg Largest County Index
4. David-Eisenburg Smallest County Index
5. Dauer-Kelsay
6. Gini

1967 Measures of Reapportionment
7. ICV
8. David-Eisenburg Largest County Index
9. David-Eisenburg Smallest County Index
10. Dauer-Kelsay

11. Actual-Ideal
12. Gini
13. Session-Lapse
14. Time-Lapse
15. Incumbency Success Ratio
16. Percent Seats Urban

Change Measures of Apportionment From 1962 to 1967
17. Δ ICV
18. Δ David-Eisenburg Largest County
19. Δ David-Eisenburg Smallest County
20. Δ Dauer-Kelsay
21. Δ Actual-Ideal
22. Δ Gini

B. Political Party Systems
   1. Inter-party Competition (Ranney)
   2. Percent Democratic Vote for Governor, 1962
   3. Legislative Party Cohesion
   4. Index of Two-Party Control (Dye)
   5. Margin of Control (Dawson-Robinson)
   6. Margin of Control, Upper House (Dye)
   7. Margin of Control, Lower House (Dye)
   8. Closeness of Competition (Dye)
   9. Inter-party Competition (Hofferbert)
   10. Extent of closeness (Dawson-Robinson)
   11. Divided Control (Dawson-Robinson)
   12. Percent Democratic Vote for Governor, 1968
   13. Change in Inter-party Competition, 1962-1967
   14. Inter-party Competition (Fenton)

C. Political Participation
   1. Voter turn-out for gubernatorial elections, 1962
   2. Legislative requirements for suffrage (Milbrath)
   3. Voter turn-out for gubernatorial elections, 1968

D. Governmental Modernism
   1. Governor's power (Schlesinger)
   2. Legislative professionalism index (Grumm)
   3. Civil service coverage

E. State Fiscal Systems
   1. Expenditure assignment, 1962
   2. Tax assignment, 1962
   3. Expenditure assignment, 1968
   4. Tax assignment, 1968

F. Political Conflict
   1. Party conflict (Francis)
   2. Pressure group conflict (Francis)

3. Regional conflict (Francis)
4. Factional conflict (Francis)
5. State-local conflict (Elazar)[6]
6. Party identification differential

G. Economic Development
1. Per capita income, 1962
2. Per capita income change (%) 1957-1962
3. Income distribution (Gini coefficient of income inequality), 1961 (Dye)
4. Industrialization, 1960
5. Education, 1960
6. Change in education, 1950-1960
7. Per capita income, 1968
8. Per capita income change (%), 1960-1968

H. Urbanism
1. Urbanization, 1960
2. Percent change in urbanization, 1950-1960
3. Percent metropolitan, 1960
4. Urbanization, 1967
5. Percent change in urbanization, 1960-1967
6. Percent metropolitan, 1966
7. Change in percent metropolitan, 1960-1966

We tried to include all the variables whose importance was evidenced in earlier studies or which we deemed to have potential importance, but we do not claim this to be an exhaustive list. The impression may be that political and governmental variables are too many and socioeconomic variables are too few to evaluate objectively their relative significance. A reading of our analytical technique will clarify why the numerical imbalance of the variables between socioeconomic, and political-governmental categories will not bias the results of our analysis.

ANALYTIC TECHNIQUE

We avoided picking a few common variables that might be significant for the explanation of all policy measures based on a priori assumptions or conceptually convincing hypotheses.[7] Rather, we developed a large pool of independent variables on the premise that the variables accounting for variance in one policy field will likely differ from the variables accounting for variance in other policy fields.[8] To accomodate this analytic approach, we used step-wise multiple regression analysis.[9] In this way, we determined the six most salient predictors for each policy measure out of the pool of independent variables, excluding our apportionment variables. We then reran each equation, adding one apportionment measure at a time. When the apportionment measure is statistically significant according to the F-test, the apportionment measure is retained in the equation; otherwise the apportionment measure does not appear in the new equation. This procedure is repeated for all appropriate apportionment measures for each policy measure. The addition of an apportionment measure in a number of cases made insignificant some of the six variables already selected through the initial run, thus eliminating them from the equations as a consequence of the second-round regression runs.[10]

This operation was originally devised to test the importance of apportionment variables as determinants of policy outcomes. However, the procedure is valid for the derivation of explanatory variables most influential in the general determination of policy variation. The reason is that adding an apportionment measure to the already selected six variables does not force the apportionment measure into the second-run regression equations, but it is only retained in the regression equation when statistically significant.[11]

We calculated four statistics expressing the relationship between the selected explanatory variables and each policy measure. They are simple correlation coefficient (r), regression coefficient, multiple correlation coefficient (R), the coefficient of multiple determination (R^2), and the portion of the R^2 that is attributable to each of the explanatory variables (ΔR^2). Since we have run as many regression equations for each policy measure as there are appropriate apportionment measures, we only used the equation that explains the policy measure best for our evaluation. Further, all those equations whose multiple correlation coefficients were below the significance level of 0.05 are excluded from consideration.

CHAPTER III
FINDINGS

The findings are presented in two parts. In the first part, the results of our regression analyses are summarized in 12 tables for the benefit of specifics. In the second part, we develop influence typology of political-governmental and socioeconomic variable categories by aggregating the findings presented in the first part.

The first part is presented in the following way: First, the tables are organized according to the types of policy measures. Second, in view of the massive volume of information and the need to conserve space, only a "barebones" summary of the findings is included in the tables. In each of the following twelve tables, column 1 shows the policy variables; column 2 the variance explained by all independent variables in the equation (R^2); columns 3 through 8 the identification of specific political-governmental variables by each of the six variable categories and the variance attributable to each specific variable (ΔR^2) in parenthesis,[12] column 9 the variance attributable to all political-governmental variables in the equation ($\frac{\Sigma \Delta R^2}{P-g}$); columns 10 and 11 the identification of specific socioeconomic variables by category and the variance attributable to each of them; and finally column 12 the variance associated to all socioeconomic variables in the equation ($\frac{\Sigma \Delta R^2}{S-e}$). Third, the findings are also organized by policy period, the 1962 findings are presented first, followed by the 1969 findings.

In presenting the first part, our attention will be focused on the general response pattern of policy variance to political-governmental and socioeconomic influences. The implications of the more significant relationships found between particular policy measures and particular explanatory variables will be the focus of our narrative.

THE 1962 RESULTS

Table 1 shows the explanatory power of the six political-governmental variable categories and two socioeconomic variable categories for the fourteen per capita spending variables. The policy variance accounted for by the selected explanatory variables exceeds 60 percent in most cases, with the extremes of the R^2s ranging from .822 for total general expenditures to only .355 for intergovernmental expenditures for education.

The comparison of columns 9 and 12 makes it apparent that per capita state expenditures are neither completely dominated by socioeconomic variables nor entirely controlled by political-governmental variables.[13] Socioeconomic variables are more influential for half of the policy variables and political-governmental variables are more influenctial for the other half. Although the evidence is not so clear-cut, the spending measures for more person-oriented services, hospitals and health, for example, are more often politics-dominated, while those for more land-oriented (or economy-oriented) services such as highways and natural resources, for example, are more frequently economics-dominated.

The measures for total expenditures and education expenditures are generally well-balanced between political and economic influences. The most important variable in these equations is state fiscal system—expenditure assignment to the state. As evidenced by earlier studies (Campbell and

[16]

TABLE 1
Relationship Between Per Capita State Expenditures and Political-Governmental and Socio-Economic Variables by Category, 1962

(1)	(2)	(3)	(4)	(5)	(6)	(7)	(8)	(9)	(10)	(11)	(12)
		Political-Governmental Variables and ΔR^2 by Variable Category							Socio-Economic Variables and ΔR^2 by Variable Category		
Policy Variables	R^2	A	B	C	D	E	F	$\sum \Delta R^2_{P-G}$	G	H	$\sum \Delta R^2_{S-E}$
Total General Expenditures	.822	4(.017)			3(.072)	1(.262)		.351	5(.332) 1(.032) 4(.067)	2(.041)	.471
Total Direct General Expenditures	.719	4(.043)	4(.055)		2(.115) 3(.029)	1(.246)		.489	1(.198)	2(.032)	.230
General Education Expenditures	.706	1(.018)			1(.054)	1(.321)		.393	5(.249)	2(.063) 1(.001)	.313
Direct Education Expenditures	.610	4(.025)				1(.207)	1(.017)	.249	5(.314) 4(.009)	2(.039)	.362
Expenditures For Higher Education	.677	1(.017)				1(.240)	1(.068)	.325	5(.258) 4(.065)	2(.029)	.352
General Highway Expenditures	.741	4(.008)	4(.003)		2(.047)	1(.010)		.068	1(.278)	3(.395)	.673

TABLE 1 (Continued)

Direct Highway Expenditures	.763	2(.006)	4(.001)	2(.022)	2(.052)			.081	1(.271) 6(.044)	3(.368)	.683
General Hospital Expenditures	.460	3(.040)		3(.246) 1(.042)			.328	1(.071) 6(.035)	3(.014) 2(.012)	.132
General Health Expenditures	.535	4(.158) 10(.052)	2(.062)	3(.073)		2(.104) 5(.073)	.522	1(.013)		.013
General Expenditures for Natural Resources	.648	4(.005)		3(.050) 2(.008)			.063	5(.272)	3(.260) 2(.049) 6(.003)	.584
General Expenditures for Correction	.695	6(.004)		3(.054)	1(.033)	4(.014)	.105	1(.416)	1(.110) 2(.065)	.591
Total Intergovern- mental Expenditures	.430	4(.139) 10(.061) 11(.029)			1(.096)	3(.086)	.411	2(.002)	1(.017)	.019
Intergovernmental Expenditures for Education	.355	3(.044)		1(.004)	1(.145)		.193	1(.061)	2(.082) 1(.019)	.162
Intergovernmental Expenditures for Highways	.370	1(.008)	4(.067) 10(.015)	1(.100)		3(.131) 2(.030) 6(.019)	.370	-	-	

Sacks, 1967; Cho, 1967), the general policy issue concerning how much the state should spend is largely determined by how much governmental service responsibility is assigned to the state government within the state-local system of government, particularly when the issue is considered from the governmental or political perspective. Our finding here also suggests that intergovernmental expenditures are primarily a function of politics and governmental characteristics although the level of variance accounted for is not high.

Legislative apportionment (malapportionment in this case) shows a strong influence over health and intergovernmental expenditures although its effect is generally weak for other spending measures. As we have noted elsewhere (Cho and Frederickson, 1973), malapportioned legislatures appear to maintain policy perspectives which are favorable to local political subdivisions either by directly assuming responsibility for particular services whose needs are not met by local governments or by providing generous financial assistance to localities which do not make their share of tax efforts. Political party systems and political participation variables are generally insignificant even for the few policy variables in which they appear.

The way the governmental modernism variables affect expenditure levels assists in understanding the legislature-governor-agency relations in budget decisions. Our findings show that legislative professionalism is inversely correlated with per capita expenditures, while governor's power and civil service coverage are positively correlated with them. This tendency suggests that strong governors and more merit-based state bureaucracies are positive influences for higher levels of spending, but more professionalized legislatures are a suppressive influence on spending levels. This finding partly modifies what Ira Sharkansky (1968) observed in his illuminating study of agency-governor-legislature role relationships in state agencies' budget success. He (1968: 1231) concludes in part that:

> The findings of greater importance for governor's recommendation (rather than agency's request) in the legislature's decisions indicates the legislature's dependence on the governor's budget cues. Perhaps this reflects the greater staff resources of the governor and the typically amateurish character of state legislatures.

What our finding indiciates is this. When the state legislature becomes more professionalized and acquires its own independent capability to review the budget, the legislature counteracts the generally expansionistic executive-bureaucracy budget policy by cutting down the appropriations. Recent innovations in an increasing number of states that have brought

[19]

greater professional capability to the legislatures seem to have strengthened their watchdog role on the public purse.[14]

Political conflict variables have a strong yet contrasting effect on a few per capita spending measures; a positive effect on total state aids and state aid for highways (regional conflict) and a negative effect on health expenditures (pressure group conflict). This finding may imply two things. First, it seems to be evident that policies of distinct substance are subject to different influences. In this case, the state policies of distributing resources among different localities are strongly affected by regional conflict, and the policy of allocating resources of benefit to a minority, the consumers of public health services, is dominated by pressure group conflict. Second, it seems to indicate that when political conflict is intense in a policy issue which is well established and occupies a prominent place in the state policy hierarchy, the resulting policy decision is made in such a way as to satisfy the conflicting or competing interests, whereas conflict on a marginal policy issue results in a denial to the proponent interests.

Economic development variables are powerful predictors of most spending level measures, a few exceptions to this being health expenditure and intergovernmental expenditures. Urbanism variables are, though generally strong, not as powerful as economic development variables. The effect of urbanism is only slight, if at all, in more than half of the equations.

Table 2 shows the relationship between the percent of change in the 11 spending measures between 1957 and 1962, and the eight categories of explanatory variables. The spending change measures are not as well explained as the spending level measures, ranging from a high of 61.8 percent for the percent change in per capita general expenditure for public welfare to a low of 30.4 percent for the percent change in per capita total intergovernmental expenditures.

Spending change policies are slightly more often (six out of eleven) dominated by governmental-political influences than socioeconomic forces as the comparison of columns 9 and 12 indicates. Political-governmental variables are a dominant influence in accounting for the change variance in direct education expenditures, public welfare expenditures, and expenditures for natural resources, whereas socioeconomic variables are the key determinants of change variance in total expenditures and highway expenditures. Political-governmental variables hold a narrow edge of balance over socioeconomic variables in accounting for the change variance in the three measures of intergovernmental expenditures.

The explanatory variable categories display a diverse pattern of relationships to the change of spending policies. Apportionment, political

TABLE 2

Relationships Between Percent Change in Per Capita State Expenditures and Political-Governmental and Socio-Economic Variables by Category, 1957-1962

(1)	(2)	(3)	(4)	(5)	(6)	(7)	(8)	(9)	(10)	(11)	(12)
		Political-Governmental Variables and ΔR^2 by Variable Category							Socio-Economic Variables and ΔR^2 by Variable Category		
Policy Variables	R^2	A	B	C	D	E	F	$\sum \Delta R^2_{P-G}$	G	H	$\sum \Delta R^2_{S-E}$
Total General Expenditures	.366	1(.002)	14(.005)		1(.075)			.082	6(.082) 5(.004)	1(.197)	.283
Total Direct Governmental Expenditures	.336	6(.002)	2(.009)		1(.069)		4(.003)	.083	6(.073) 5(.000)	1(.180)	.253
General Education Expenditures	.334	1(.010)	8(.029)		3(.079)		4(.045)	.163	6(.083) 4(.043) 5(.045)		.171
Direct Education Expenditures	.349	5(.002)	4(.111)	1(.064)	1(.099)		1(.045)	.321	1(.020)	1(.008)	.028
General Highway Expenditures	.418	5(.007)	10(.014) 4(.002)				4(.003)	.026	4(.230)	3(.163)	.393
Direct Highway Expenditures	.436	5(.007)	10(.008) 4(.002)				4(.005)	.022	4(.233) 6(.013)	3(.170)	.416
Public Welfare Expenditures	.618	4(.085)	8(.075)		2(.167)		5(.077)	.405	5(.213)	2(.000)	.213
General Expenditures for Natural Resources	.326	5(.044)			2(.071) 1(.037)	1(.019)	3(.102)	.272	4(.036)	3(.018)	.054
Total Intergovernmental Expenditures	.304	6(.005)	8(.085) 4(.069)	1(.020)				.179	5(.044) 1(.048)	1(.033)	.125
Intergovernmental Expenditures for Education	.525	4(.017)	4(.062)	1(.189)				.268	5(.101) 4(.073) 2(.021)	1(.062)	.257
Intergovernmental Expenditures for Highways	.614	1(.024)				1(.245)	5(.042)	.311	4(.140) 5(.055) 6(.074) 6(.035)		.304

participation, governmental modernism, economic development, and urbanism influence the spending policy changes in a similar way as they did the spending level decisions. However, political party system, and political conflict variables influence the spending change variance more often and more strongly than in the spending level variance equations. The influence of state fiscal system is also drastically different, intergovernmental expenditure for highways being the only policy measure strongly affected by expenditure assignment.

In general, the decisions as to how fast the state should increase its spending levels are more often determined by political considerations than economic considerations, though the difference is slight.

The tax level variance accounted for by the selected explanatory variables is generally high as shown in Table 3. The R^2 s range from the high of .849 for total taxes to the low of .365 for sales taxes. The tax level variance is in the main a function of economic differences among the states. This finding confirms the conclusions of many earlier studies (Dye, 1966). It seems that the level of state tax yields is largely a tautological phenomenon in that richer states raise more taxes and poorer states raise less. Sales taxes are the only exception to this generalization. As often discussed, sales taxes are more susceptible to political manipulation than other state taxes—say, income taxes. The consumers as taxpayers are less resistant to sales taxes than to personal income taxes because they generally consider the taxes are a part of the cost of the purchases.[15]

Changes in tax policies are highly politicized as Table 4 shows. All but property tax change are primarily determined by the differences in political-governmental character, and economic differences are only a minor influence. In fact, a report by Advisory Commission on Intergovernmental Relations (1966) shows that the tax rate changes made by legislative enactment have generally contributed more to the increase in state tax revenues during the 1950-1967 period than has economic growth.

Table 5 shows the effect of the selected explanatory variables on the five distribution policies of state spending between metropolitan and nonmetropolitan areas. It has been a long-standing argument that the rural bias of state fund distribution is caused by malapportioned legislatures.[16] However, our findings show that malapportionment per se is not a dominant factor in determining the metropolitan-nonmetropolitan disparity in state distribution policies. It has only a minor impact on the spending distribution for highways and public welfare. In general, political and governmental differences explain better the rural bias of school aid distribution and state direct control of road mileages, whereas economic development and urbanism are more dominant influences in accounting

[22]

TABLE 3
Relationships Between Per Capita State Taxes and Political-Governmental and Socio-Economic Variables by Category, 1962

(1)	(2)	(3)	(4)	(5)	(6)	(7)	(8)	(9)	(10)	(11)	(12)
		Political-Governmental Variables and ΔR^2 by Variable Category							Socio-Economic Variables and ΔR^2 by Variable Category		
Policy Variables	R^2	A	B	C	D	E	F	$\sum \Delta R^2_{P-G}$	G	H	$\sum \Delta R^2_{S-E}$
Total Taxes	.849	1(.020)	4(.051)			2(.295)		.366	1(.468) 5(.015)		.483
Total Sales Taxes	.365	1(.039)	2(.020)	2(.029)		2(.151)	1(.101)	.340	6(.003)	2(.022)	.025
Income Taxes	.601	3(.016)	11(.017) 10(.038)					.071	1(.320) 2(.025)	2(.185)	.530
Property Taxes	.569	5(.035)					4(.128) 3(.081)	.244	5(.156) 1(.121)	2(.047)	.324

TABLE 4
Relationships Between Percent Change in Per Capita State Taxes and Political-Governmental and Socio-Economic Variables by Category, 1957-1962

(1)	(2)	(3)	(4)	(5)	(6)	(7)	(8)	(9)	(10)	(11)	(12)
		Political-Governmental Variables and ΔR^2 by Variable Category							Socio-Economic Variables and ΔR^2 by Variable Category		
Policy Variables	R^2	A	B	C	D	E	F	$\sum \Delta R^2_{P-G}$	G	H	$\sum \Delta R^2_{S-E}$
Total Taxes	.442	4(.019)		1(.100)	1(.038)		6(.162) 3(.040)	.359	1(.020) 5(.062)		.082
Total Sales Taxes	.379	4(.029)	8(.146) 10(.041)	2(.032)	2(.027)			.275	5(.066) 6(.038)		.104
Income Taxes	.402	1(.067)			3(.045) 2(.045)	2(.147)	2(.021)	.325	4(.043) 5(.033)		.076
Property Taxes	.319	4(.003)	4(.081)					.084	1(.180) 6(.012) 3(.001)	1(.043)	.326

for the highway spending and welfare spending disparities. Our finding suggests that regional conflict is a strong influence countering the rural bias of welfare spending.

Politics is more influential than economics in affecting state redistributive policy for lower income groups. Although the extent of variance explained is modest, this finding, as shown in Table 6, confirms what Fry-Winters (1970) found in their earlier study.[17]

The pattern that emerges from the 1962 analysis is highly illustrative of the complexity of the fiscal decision-making process. The economic and social character of a state seems to be the dominant influence over how much it spends in total and how much it taxes generally. This may be mostly tautological—how wealthy a state is determines the size of the state budget. But political and governmental factors are not unimportant in total expenditures and general tax decisions, particularly important is expenditure and tax assignment.

Decisions as to how much of the state budget is to be devoted to each function exhibit patterns of mixed dominance; some are controlled more by socioeconomic influence and others are dominated by political and governmental influences. State aid policies to lesser jurisdictions and expenditures for emerging social services, such as health and hospitals, are more politics-dominated decisions, whereas expenditures for highways and natural resources are more economics-dominated policy decisions. It seems to indicate that the change of social and economic conditions by itself does not reorient public policies, but political recognition of change in attitudes or conditions and the resulting political actions to accommodate to change can effect policy.

State distribution policies between geographical regions and redistributive policy between income classes are decisions about equally shared political-governmental and socioeconomic influences.

THE 1967-1969 RESULTS

The relationship of the fourteen per capita spending measures in 1969 to the most powerful political and economic variables are summarized in Table 7. The R^2s range from a high of .763 for per capita total direct expenditures to a low of .455 for per capita intergovernmental expenditure for highways. In the fourteen equations, it is politics, not economics, that mainly determines all but four of the spending level measures. In the remaining three of the four measures, political influence is nearly as great as economic impact.

Perhaps the most interesting finding here is that there is a complete shift in the influence on total highway expenditures. In 1962 both general and direct expenditures for highways are nearly entirely determined by socioeconomic influences, especially urbanism and metropolitanism variables, but in 1969 politics is exclusively responsible for their variance. Why has this drastic shift occurred? One important reason seems to lie in state involvement in the Interstate Highway System development which is mostly financed by federal funding. In the early part of the 1960s, the I-System development was still in the initial stage and its construction was mainly concentrated in the rural part of the states. The projects then were largely economy-stimulating and politically noncontroversial from the state point of view and speedy progress took place in the rural states. However, as the development of the I-System progressed and reached the stage of large-scale construction of its urban extensions in the metropolitan areas in the late part of the 1960s, political controversies erupted regarding the route selections and designs and their impact on urban residential disintegration of ghetto neighborhoods and on commercial and industrial interests. the dominant influence of legislative professionalism and political participation on the 1969 highway expenditures seems to reflect, to a significant degree, the changed political context in which the Interstate Highway System had been moved.

Politics is even more influential in the determination of spending changes from 1962 to 1969 than in determining 1969 spending levels. As shown in Table 8, politics mostly determines the pattern of spending changes in all but one of the eleven examined measures. Even for the single exception, percent change of per capita public welfare spending, political-governmental variables account for 44.2 percent of the explained variance.

Table 9 shows that the six selected explanatory variables account for 81.3 percent of the interstate variation in per capita total taxes in 1969. The three political variables account for 60.9 percent of the explained portion of the per capita tax variance.

As Table 10 shows, the change pattern in taxing policies from 1962 to 1969 is also primarily determined by politics.

The pattern of the states' distribution between metropolitan and nonmetropolitan areas is modestly influenced by politics compared with other policy measures. As Table 11 indicates, three of the six distributive measures (total state aid, state aid to schools, and road mileage under state control) are more influenced by political variables, while state highway expenditure, state-local welfare expenditure, and state direct welfare expenditures are more economically determined.

Finally, the state and local redistributive policy for lower income groups is primarily the result of political and governmental influence. Of

TABLE 5
Relationships Between Metro-Nonmetro Ratio of Per Capita State Expenditures and Political-Governmental and Socio-Economic Variables by Category, 1962

(1)	(2)	(3)	(4)	(5)	(6)	(7)	(8)	(9)	(10)	(11)	(12)
		Political-Governmental Variables and ΔR^2 by Variable Category							Socio-Economic Variables and ΔR^2 by Variable Category		
Policy Variables	R^2	A	B	C	D	E	F	$\sum \Delta R^2_{P-G}$	G	H	$\sum \Delta R^2_{S-E}$
School Aid Per Pupil	.620	1(.010)	2(.094) 10(.055) 8(.146)	1(.083)				.338	2(.131)	2(.101)	.232
State Highway Expenditures	.576	3(.064)	2(.005)	1(.047)				.116	1(.127) 6(.096)	2(.201) 3(.035)	.459
State-Local Welfare Expenditures	.539	3(.020)					3(.107)	.127	3(.412)		.412
State Direct Expenditures for Welfare	.667	6(.007)					3(.157)	.164	3(.445)	3(.059)	.504
Road Mileage Under State Control	.479	5(.031)	4(.049) 8(.135)				4(.045)	.261	4(.141) 5(.008)	2(.069)	.218

TABLE 6
Relationships Between the Expenditure Benefits-Tax Burdens Ratio for Lower Income Groups and Political-Governmental and Socio-Economic Variables by Category, 1961

(1)	(2)	(3)	(4)	(5)	(6)	(7)	(8)	(9)	(10)	(11)	(12)
		\multicolumn{6}{c}{Political-Governmental Variables and ΔR^2 by Variable Category}		$\sum \Delta R^2$ P-G	\multicolumn{3}{c}{Socio-Economic Variables and ΔR^2 by Variable Category}	
Policy Variables	R^2	A	B	C	D	E	F		G	H	$\sum \Delta R^2$ S-E
The Expenditure Benefit-Tax Burden Ratio, 1961	.351	4(.037)	5(.024)		3(.043) 2(.095)			.200	6(.026) 3(.086)	2(.039)	.151

TABLE 7
Relationships Between Per Capita Expenditures and Political-Governmental and Socio-Economic Variables by Category, 1969

(1)	(2)	(3)	(4)	(5)	(6)	(7)	(8)	(9)	(10)	(11)	(12)
		Political-Governmental Variables and ΔR^2 by Variable Category							Socio-Economic Variables and ΔR^2 by Variable Category		
Policy Variables	R^2	A	B	C	D	E	F	$\sum \Delta R^2_{P-G}$	G	H	$\sum \Delta R^2_{S-E}$
Total General Expenditures	.591	19(.033)	8(.031)			3(.163)	5(.030)	.257	5(.320)	7(.007) 2(.007)	.334
Total Direct General Expenditures	.763	15(.033)	4(.128)			3(.131)	5(.216)	.507	8(.120) 4(.063)	7(.073)	.256
General Education Expenditures	.546	17(.036)			3(.020)	3(.176)		.232	5(.259)	7(.055)	.314
Expenditures for Higher Education	.644	12(.027)		3(.020)		3(.194)	6(.020)	.261	5(.204) 4(.163)	4(.016)	.383
General Highway Expenditures	.674	10(.073)	14(.208)	2(.021)	2(.314)		4(.037) 3(.017) 5(.006)	.674	–	–	–

TABLE 7 (Continued)

Direct Highway Expenditures	.636	—	—				3(.021)/1(.015)	.636	—	—	—
Public Welfare Expenditures	.478	7(.051)	14(.142)		2(.277)	3(.130)		.379	4(.046)	4(.053)	.099
General Hospital Expenditures	.564	21(.008)		3(.079)	2(.254)/1(.002)	3(.036)		.437	6(.127)		.127
General Health Expenditures	.616	20(.104)	12(.020)/5(.011)	3(.193)	2(.034)		3(.075)	.396	4(.207)	6(.013)	.220
General Expenditures For Natural Resources	.687	7(.057)		3(.143)/2(.057)			5(.098)/2(.041)	.194	5(.181)	6(.312)	.493
General Expenditures For Corrections	.703	15(.019)/10(.023)	11(.031)/10(.023)				3(.079)/5(.041)	.358	7(.345)		.345
Total Intergovernmental Expenditures	.570	8(.023)		2(.007)	2(.045)	3(.284)		.515	7(.055)		.055
Intergovernmental Expenditures for Education	.614	17(.148)	13(.020)	3(.282)	1(.003)	3(.045)	2(.020)	.611		4(.003)	.003
Intergovernmental Expenditures for Highways	.455	21(.272)/13(.014)	12(.111)/13(.014)			3(.211)	2(.161)/3(.058)	.335	8(.065)/5(.055)		.120

[29]

TABLE 8
Relationships Between Percent Change in Per Capita State Expenditures and Political-Governmental and Socio-Economic Variables by Category, 1962-1969

(1)	(2)	(3)	(4)	(5)	(6)	(7)	(8)	(9)	(10)	(11)	(12)
		\multicolumn{6}{c}{Political-Governmental Variables and ΔR^2 by Variable Category}		\multicolumn{3}{c}{Socio-Economic Variables and ΔR^2 by Variable Category}	
Policy Variables	R^2	A	B	C	D	E	F	$\sum \Delta R^2_{P-G}$	G	H	$\sum \Delta R^2_{S-E}$
Total General Expenditures	.562	15(.018)	12(.043)	3(.310)	3(.039)		5(.045)	.455	6(.025)	7(.082)	.107
Total Direct General Expenditures	.446	14(.087)			1(.034)		1(.223) 5(.055)	.398	6(.029) 5(.008) 8(.011)		.048
General Education Expenditures	.608	14(.096)		3(.073)			5(.130) 1(.051) 6(.031)	.380	5(.013)	7(.215)	.228
Expenditures for Higher Education	.415	14(.166)	10(.026) 11(.049) 15(.024) 8(.032)				5(.111)	.408	3(.007)		.007
General Highway Expenditures	.349	7(.075)	8(.037)		1(.036) 2(.018)		1(.163)	.329	7(.020)		.020
Direct Highway Expenditures	.511	10(.030)	10(.117) 4(.038) 8(.111)		1(.054)		1(.161)	.510	7(.001)		.001
Public Welfare Expenditures	.659	10(.067)	4(.012) 13(.014)	3(.130)		3(.011)	6(.057)	.291	7(.368)		.368
General Hospital Expenditures	.366	7(.017)	12(.042)	3(.046) 2(.045)	3(.060)	3(.115)	2(.041)	.366		-	-
General Health Expenditures	.372	20(.114)	4(.056)	2(.031)			3(.028) 1(.019) 6(.116)	.364	3(.008)		.008
General Expenditures For Natural Resources	.409	8(.018)	11(.009)		3(.088) 2(.131)			.246	8(.019)	7(.102) 4(.042)	.163
Total Intergovernmental Expenditures	.445	14(.078)	12(.055) 10(.040)	3(.163)		3(.001)		.337	4(.064)	7(.044)	.108

TABLE 9
Relationships Between Per Capita State Taxes and Political-Governmental and Socio-Economic Variables by Category, 1969

(1)	(2)	(3)	(4)	(5)	(6)	(7)	(8)	(9)	(10)	(11)	(12)
		Political-Governmental Variables and ΔR^2 by Variable Category							Socio-Economic Variables and ΔR^2 by Variable Category		
Policy Variables	R^2	A	B	C	D	E	F	$\sum \Delta R^2_{P-G}$	G	H	$\sum \Delta R^2_{S-E}$
Total Taxes	.813	7(.008)		3(.025)		4(.462)		.495	7(.230) 5(.054) 4(.034)		.318

TABLE 10
Relationships Between Percent Change in Per Capita State Taxes and Political-Governmental and Socio-Economic Variables by Category, 1962-1969

(1)	(2)	(3)	(4)	(5)	(6)	(7)	(8)	(9)	(10)	(11)	(12)
		Political-Governmental Variables and ΔR^2 by Variable Category							Socio-Economic Variables and ΔR^2 by Variable Category		
Policy Variables	R^2	A	B	C	D	E	F	$\sum \Delta R^2_{P-G}$	G	H	$\sum \Delta R^2_{S-E}$
Total Taxes	.446	16(.051)	12(.176) 11(.031)		1(.059)		5(.035) 2(.037)	.389	8(.057)		.057
Total Sales Taxes	.423	11(.034)		3(.032)	2(.056)	4(.136)	4(.039)	.297	6(.029)	5(.097)	.126

TABLE 11
Relationships Between Metro-Nonmetro Ratio of Per Capita State Expenditures and Political-Governmental and Socio-Economic Variables by Category, 1967

(1)	(2)	(3)	(4)	(5)	(6)	(7)	(8)	(9)	(10)	(11)	(12)
		Political-Governmental Variables and ΔR^2 by Variable Category							Socio-Economic Variables and ΔR^2 by Variable Category		
Policy Variables	R^2	A	B	C	D	E	F	$\sum \Delta R^2_{P-G}$	G	H	$\sum \Delta R^2_{S-E}$
Total State Aid	.514	19(.184)		2(.036) 3(.031)			5(.031)	.282	5(.026) 3(.002)	5(.204)	.232
School Aid Per Pupil	.271	18(.145)					3(.005)	.150	5(.020) 3(.027)	5(.074)	.121
State-Local Welfare Expenditures	.575	16(.046)		3(.066)	3(.035)		4(.034)	.181	3(.367)	4(.027)	.394
State Direct Welfare Expenditures	.754	8(.025)	4(.051)				2(.066) 6(.041)	.183	3(.502)	6(.032)	.572
State Highway Expenditures	.690	19(.006)						.006	5(.104) 4(.027) 8(.029)	6(.467) 5(.035) 4(.022)	.684
Road Mileage Under State Control	.495	19(.113)	4(.074) 8(.188) 11(.092)	2(.014)				.481	4(.008)	4(.008)	.016

[34]

TABLE 12
Relationships Between the Expenditure Benefit-Tax Burden Ratio for Lower Income Groups and Political-Governmental and Socio-Economic Variables by Category, 1967

(1)	(2)	(3)	(4)	(5)	(6)	(7)	(8)	(9)	(10)	(11)	(12)
		Political-Governmental Variables and ΔR^2 by Variable Category							Socio-Economic Variables and ΔR^2 by Variable Category		
Policy Variables	R^2	A	B	C	D	E	F	$\sum \Delta R^2_{P-G}$	G	H	$\sum \Delta R^2_{S-E}$
The Expenditure Benefit – Tax Burden Ratio 1967	.466	15(.031)	12(.162) 8(.039)		2(.069)		5(.099) 4(.036)	.436	6(.030)		.030

the 46.6 percent of the variance explained, as shown in Table 12, 43.6 percent is accounted for by six political-governmental variables, while the remaining 3 percent is explained by an educational change variable.

The 1969 spending equations display essentially the same pattern as the 1962 equations although spending decisions in most functions are more political in 1969 than they were in 1962. The extreme example of this is the total highway spending case discussed above. The same direction is seen in aid to education.

Again the dominant pattern is economic and social factors controlling the size of the state pie, looking at that pie particularly from the spending angle. Yet, how much spending is to be done in the "locality related" functions (education, health, hospitals, total aid and aid for education and highways, and redistribution) is still dominated by political and governmental forces.

CHAPTER IV
INFLUENCE TYPOLOGY OF POLICY DETERMINANTS

SYNTHESIS

The methods used for organizing the twelve preceding tables to present our findings include a number of innovations. As in the traditional form of presentation, the effect of independent variables on each policy measure is presented for each specific independent variable, but it is presented by category of independent variables. Second, the effect of independent variables is aggregated for the six political-governmental variable categories and for the two socioeconomic variable categories.

However, this form of presentation is too complex to ascertain the general pattern of influence relationships between diverse categories of independent variables and various groups of policy measures either at a particular point of time or over a period of time span. For example, the general pattern of influence of the eight categories of independent variables on the entire range of policy measures is not readily apparent for a systematic comparison at one policy period. Nor are the changes in the general pattern of their influence on the entire range of policy measures from one policy period to the other readily specifiable.

What is needed to overcome this difficulty is to devise a conceptual scheme to synthesize the outcomes of our analyses in such a way as to elicit the general pattern of influence of any category of independent variables on any groups of policy measures. Our attempt here is to develop such a conceptual scheme which is appropriate for classifying an influence typology of the eight categories of independent variables on any groupings of policy variables. We employ two-dimensional influence criteria, scope and intensity of influence. The scope of influence is to define the range of the policy span in which each independent variable category bears a degree of influence. The intensity of influence is to determine the strength of the influence of any independent variable categories within a defined range of policy measures. These influence criteria make it possible to remove the consideration of the policy impact pattern of a given independent variable category from a specific policy variable and place it on the entire range of policy areas or policy sub-groups.

The measurement of the influence scope and influence intensity is operationalized in the following way. The influence scope is measured by the relationship between the frequency of different policy variables in which a particular independent variable category shows influence and the total number of policy measures considered. The influence intensity is determined by the relationship between the average influence of a given independent variable category and the average influence of the most powerful independent variable category. The scope and intensity of influence are divided into three scales each: extensive (E), medium (M), and narrow (N) for the influence scope; and strong (S), moderate (M), and weak (W) for the influence intensity. The methods and procedures devised for the computation of the scales of the two influence criteria are described in detail in the following two sections.

THE SCOPE OF INFLUENCE

The scope of influence of a particular independent variable category represents the number of policy measures influenced by that variable category within a given group of policy measures. The general concept of influence scope, therefore, can be expressed by an equation as follows:

$$SI(vi) = P_n(vi) \quad \quad \quad \quad \quad \quad (1)$$

Where: vi represents a particular independent variable category, i.e., A, B, C, D, E, F, G, or H as the independent variables are categorized in our study; SI represents the scope of influence; thus, SI(vi) represents the scope of influence for the independent variable category, vi; P_n represents a particular group (n) of policy measures (P) such as all measures of fiscal policy or the spending level measures of fiscal policy; and $P_n(vi)$ represents the number of policy measures (P) influenced by the independent variable category, vi, of the n policy group.

The scale of influence scope of a particular independent variable category is the number of policy measures influenced by that variable category as a function (f) of the total number of policy measures included in a policy group for which the influence typology is considered. This relationship can be written in an equation as:

$$Pn(vi) = f(Pn) \qquad (2)$$

Where: Pn represents the total number of policy measures (P) included in a policy group (n) for which the influence typology is considered.

The specific scales of influence scope (E, M, and N) are determined by a set of relationships between Pn(vi) and Pn as follows:

$$SI(vi) = E \text{ when } Pn(vi) > 2/3 \text{ (Pn)} \qquad (3)$$
$$SI(vi) = M \text{ when } Pn(vi) \leqslant 2/3 \text{ (Pn), but } Pn(vi) > 1/3 \text{ (Pn)} \qquad (4)$$
$$SI(vi) = N \text{ when } Pn(vi) \leqslant 1/3 \text{ (Pn)} \qquad (5)$$

Table 13 presents the frequency of policy measures influenced by the eight categories of independent variables in terms of the six policy areas and all policy areas combined for each policy period and all policy areas combined for the two policy periods. By substituting the information presented in Equations 3, 4, and 5, we can compute the scale of influence scope for any independent variable categories for any policy groups. For example, the scale of influence scope for any independent variable category for the policy group of all policy measures in the 1969 policy period can be determined as follows:

Since Pn = 35:
$SI(vi) = E$ when $Pn(vi) > 2/3$ x (35), i.e., $Pn(vi) > 24$;
$SI(vi) = M$ when $Pn(vi) \leqslant 2/3$ x (35), but $Pn(vi) > 1/3$ x (35), i.e., $Pn(vi) \leqslant 24$, but > 12; and
$SI(vi) = N$ when $Pn(vi) \leqslant 1/3$ x (35), i.e., $Pn(vi) \leqslant 12$.

Therefore, the scale of influence scope for the eight independent variable categories, A, B, C, D, E, F, G, and H for the policy group of all policy measures in the 1969 policy period is as follows:

Apportionment measures (A);
$SI(va) = E$ because $Pn(va) = 35$ and $Pn(va) > 24$.

TABLE 13
Frequency of Influence of Independent Variables Categories by Fiscal Policy Areas

Fiscal Policy Area	Number of Equations	A	B	C	D	E	F	G	H
1962:									
1. P.C. Expenditures, 1962	14	14	6	3	10	9	6	13	12
2. Percent change, P.C. Expenditures, 1957-1962	11	11	9	3	6	2	8	11	9
3. Per Capita State Taxes, 1962	4	4	3	1	0	2	2	4	3
4. Percent change in P.C. taxes, 1957-1962	4	4	2	2	3	1	2	4	1
5. Metro-Nonmetro state spending distribution, 1962	5	5	3	2	0	0	3	5	4
6. Ratio, state expenditure benefit to tax burdens for lower income groups, 1961	1	1	1	0	1	0	0	1	1
Subtotal	39	39	24	11	20	14	21	39	29
1967/1969									
7. P.C. expenditures, 1969	14	14	9	7	7	9	10	11	8
8. Percent change, P.C. Expenditures, 1962-1969	11	11	9	6	6	3	9	10	4
9. Per Capita State Taxes, 1969	1	1	0	1	0	1	0	1	0
10. Percent change, P.C. Taxes, 1962-1969	2	2	1	1	2	1	2	2	1
11. Metro-Nonmetro State spending distribution, 1967	6	6	2	3	1	0	4	6	6
12. Ratio, State-Local Expenditures Benefits to Tax Burdens for Lower Income Groups, 1967	1	1	1	0	1	0	1	1	0
Subtotal	35	35	22	18	17	14	26	34	19
Total	74	74	46	29	37	28	47	73	48

Political party systems (B);
SI(vb) = M because Pn(vb) = 22 and Pn(vb) < 24, but > 12.
Political participation variables (C);
SI(vc) = M because Pn(vc) = 18 and Pn(vc) < 24, but > 12.
Governmental modernism variables (D);
SI(vd) = M because Pn(vd) = 17 and Pn(vd) < 24, but > 12.
State fiscal systems variables (E);
SI(ve) = M because Pn(ve) = 14 and Pn(ve) < 24, but > 12.
Political conflict variables (F);
SI(vf) = E because Pn(vf) = 26 and Pn(vf) > 24.
Economic development varibles (G);
SI(vg) = E because Pn(vg) = 34 and Pn(vg) > 24.
Urbanism variables (H);
SI(vh) = M because Pn(vh) = 19 and Pn(vh) < 24, but > 12.

THE INTENSITY OF INFLUENCE

The intensity of influence represents the average explanatory power of an independent variable category for policy measures of a particular policy group. Thus, the general concept of influence intensity can be expressed by an equation as follows:

$$II(vi) = f \frac{\Sigma \Delta R^2 Pn(vi)}{Pn(vi)} \quad \quad \quad \quad \quad (6)$$

Where: vi represents a particular independent variable category: II(vi), thus, represents the intensity of influence of the variable category, vi; Pn(vi), then, represents the policy measures (P) included in the policy group, n, influenced by the independent variable category, vi; and $\Sigma \Delta R^2 Pn(vi)$ represents the sum of the percent variance in policy measures, Pn, accounted for by the independent variable category, vi.

The scale of influence intensity is determined by the average explanatory power of a particular independent variable category as a function (f) of the average explanatory power of the most powerful independent variable category for all policy measures in all policy periods (two policy periods in our case) combined. Therefore, the relationship of explanatory power that determines the scale of influence intensity, S, M, or W can be written into an equation as follows:

[40]

$$\frac{\Sigma \Delta R^2 Pn(vi)}{Pn(vi)} = f \left\{ \frac{[\Sigma \Delta R^2 PN(vm),t_1 + \Sigma \Delta R^2 PN(vm),t_2]}{[PN(vm),t_1] + [PN(vm),t_2]} \right\} \quad \ldots \quad (7)$$

Where: vm represents the most powerful independent variable category; PN represents the policy measures (P) of all policy groups (N); and t_1 and t_2 represent the policy periods 1 and 2, respectively.

Thus, whether the scale of influence intensity of a particular independent variable category is S, M, or W is determined as follows:

II(vi) = S when

$$\frac{\Sigma \Delta R^2 Pn(vi)}{Pn(vi)} > 2/3 \times \left\{ \frac{[\Sigma \Delta R^2 PN(vm),t_1] + [\Sigma \Delta R^2 PN(vm),t_2]}{[PN(vm),t_1] + [PN(vm),t_2]} \right\} \quad .\,.(8)$$

II(vi) = M when,

$$\frac{\Sigma \Delta R^2 pn(vi)}{Pn(vi)} \leqslant 2/3 \times \left\{ \frac{[\Sigma \Delta R^2 PN(vm),t_1] + [\Sigma \Delta R^2 PN(vm),t_2]}{[PN(vm),t_1] + [PN(vm),t_2]} \right\} \text{ but}$$

$$> 1/3 \times \left\{ \frac{[\Sigma \Delta R^2 PN(vm),t_1] + [\Sigma \Delta R^2 PN(vm),t_2]}{[PN(vm),t_1] + [PN(vm),t_2]} \right\} \quad .\,.(9)$$

II(vi) = W when

$$\frac{\Sigma \Delta R^2 PN(vi)}{Pn(vi)} \leqslant 1/3 \times \left\{ \frac{[\Sigma \Delta R^2 PN(vm),t_1] + [\Sigma \Delta R^2 PN(vm),t_2]}{[PN(vm),t_1] + [PN(vm),t_2]} \right\} \quad . \quad (10)$$

Table 14 presents the average explanatory power of each of the eight independent variable categories for all policy measures combined and for each of the six policy areas in each policy period and for all policy measures of the two policy periods combined. The average explanatory power for all policy measures of the two policy periods combined is most powerful for the independent variable category, G, i.e., economic development variable category.

When vg is substituted for vm,

$$\frac{[\Sigma \Delta R^2 PN(vg),t_1] + [\Sigma \Delta R^2 PN(vg),t_2]}{[PN(vg),t_1] + [PN(vg),t_2]} = .165 \;.$$

Therefore, whether the scale of influence intensity for a particular independent variable category is S, M, or W can be determined as follows:

II(vi) = S when,

$$\frac{\Sigma \Delta R^2 Pn(vi)}{Pn(vi)} > 2/3 \times (.165), \text{ i.e., } \frac{\Sigma \Delta R^2 Pn(vi)}{Pn(vi)} > (.110) \;.$$

II(vi) = M when,

$$\frac{\Sigma\Delta R^2 Pn(vi)}{Pn(vi)} \leqslant 2/3 \times (.165), \text{ but } > 1/3 \times (.165), \text{ i.e.,}$$

$$\frac{\Sigma\Delta R^2 Pn(vi)}{Pn(vi)} \leqslant (.110), \text{ but } > (.055).$$

II(vi) = W when,

$$\frac{\Sigma\Delta R^2 Pn(vi)}{Pn(vi)} \leqslant 1/3 \times (.165), \text{ i.e., } \frac{\Sigma\Delta R^2 Pn(vi)}{Pn(vi)} \leqslant (.055).$$

By substituting the information presented in Table 14 for the corresponding terms in the Equations 8, 9, and 10, we can compute the scale of influence intensity of the eight independent variable categories for any policy groups. For example, the scales of influence intensity of the eight independent variable categories for all policy measures in the 1969 policy periods are as follows:

Apportionment measures (A);

$$II(va) = M \text{ because } \frac{\Sigma\Delta R^2 Pn(va)}{Pn(va)} = (.066) \text{ and}$$

$$\frac{\Sigma\Delta R^2 Pn(va)}{Pn(va)} < (.110), \text{ but } > (.055).$$

Political party systems variables (B);

$$II(vb) = M \text{ because } \frac{\Sigma\Delta R^2 Pn(vb)}{Pn(vb)} = (.107) \text{ and}$$

$$\frac{\Sigma\Delta R^2 Pn(vb)}{Pn(vb)} < (.110), \text{ but } > (.055).$$

Political participation variables (C);

$$II(vc) = M \text{ because } \frac{\Sigma\Delta R^2 Pn(vc)}{Pn(vc)} = (.100) \text{ and}$$

$$\frac{\Sigma\Delta R^2 Pn(vc)}{Pn(vc)} < (.110), \text{ but } > (.055).$$

Governmental modernism variables (D);

$$II(vd) = M \text{ because } \frac{\Sigma\Delta R^2 Pn(vd)}{Pn(vd)} = (.096) \text{ and}$$

$$\frac{\Sigma\Delta R^2 Pn(vd)}{Pn(vd)} < (.110), \text{ but } > (.055).$$

TABLE 14
Average Explanatory Power of Independent Variable Categories by Fiscal Policy Areas

Fiscal Policy Area	A	B	C	D	E	F	G	H
1962:								
1. Per Capita Expenditures, 1962	.038	.047	.061	.085	.173	.090	.230	.133
2. Percent Change, P.C. Expenditures, 1957-1962	.019	.052	.091	.100	.132	.040	.151	.092
3. Per Capita State Taxes, 1962	.027	.042	.029	-	.223	.155	.277	.085
4. Percent Change, P.C. State Taxes, 1957-1962	.030	.089	.066	.052	.147	.112	.114	.043
5. Metro-Nonmetro State Spending Distribution, 1962	.026	.161	.065	-	-	.103	.272	.093
6. Ratio, State Expenditure Benefits to Tax Burdens for Lower Income Groups, 1961	.037	.024	-	.138	-	-	.112	.039
Subtotal	.029	.069	.068	.087	.173	.081	.197	.114
1967-1969								
7. Per Capita Expenditures, 1969	.065	.092	.115	.136	.152	.094	.201	.067
8. Percent Change, P.C. Expenditures, 1962-1969	.070	.078	.133	.077	.042	.137	.057	.121
9. Per Capita State Taxes, 1969	.008	-	.025	-	.462	-	.318	-
10. Percent Change, P.C. Taxes, 1962-1969	.043	.207	.032	.058	.136	.056	.043	.097
11. Metro-Nonmetro State Spending Distribution, 1967	.087	.202	.049	.035	-	.044	.185	.145
12. Ratio, State-Local Expenditure Benefits To State-Local Tax Burdens for Lower Income Groups, 1967	.031	.201	-	.009	-	.135	.030	-
Subtotal	.066	.107	.100	.096	.150	.100	.127	.105
Total	.046	.087	.088	.091	.161	.091	.165	.109

State fiscal systems variables (E);

$\mathrm{II(ve)} = \mathrm{S}$ because $\dfrac{\Sigma \Delta R^2 \mathrm{Pn(ve)}}{\mathrm{Pn(ve)}} = (.150)$ and

$\dfrac{\Sigma \Delta R^2 \mathrm{Pn(ve)}}{\mathrm{Pn(ve)}} > (.110)$.

Political conflict variables (F);

$\mathrm{II(vf)} = \mathrm{M}$ because $\dfrac{\Sigma \Delta R^2 \mathrm{Pn(vf)}}{\mathrm{Pn(vf)}} = (.100)$ and

$\dfrac{\Sigma \Delta R^2 \mathrm{Pn(vf)}}{\mathrm{Pn(vf)}} < (.110)$, but $> (.055)$.

Economic development variables (G);

$\mathrm{II(vg)} = \mathrm{S}$ because $\dfrac{\Sigma \Delta R^2 \mathrm{Pn(vg)}}{\mathrm{Pn(vg)}} = (.127)$ and

$\dfrac{\Sigma \Delta R^2 \mathrm{Pn(vg)}}{\mathrm{Pn(vg)}} > (.110)$.

Urbanism variables (H);

$\mathrm{II(vh)} = \mathrm{M}$ because $\dfrac{\Sigma \Delta R^2 \mathrm{Pn(vh)}}{\mathrm{Pn(vh)}} = (.105)$ and

$\dfrac{\Sigma \Delta R^2 \mathrm{Pn(vh)}}{\mathrm{Pn(vh)}} < (.110)$, but $> (.055)$.

TYPOLOGY OF INFLUENCE

The scales of influence are devised differently for the two influence criteria. For the scope of influence, the scales are devised in such a way that there can be as many sets of scales of influence scope as there are policy groups for which influence typology is desired. However, only a single set of scales of influence intensity is stipulated. The reason for doing this is simply to make the typology of influence comparable whether the influence pattern of independent variable categories is compared for different policy groups within the same policy period or for different as well as same policy groups between different policy periods.

By coordinating the scales of the two influence criteria, namely, the scales of influence scope on the Y axis and the scales of influence intensity on the X axis, we can map the influence of any given independent variable category into nine types: extensive-strong (E-S), extensive-moderate (E-M), extensive-weak (E-W), medium—strong (M-S), medium-moderate (M-M), medium-weak (M-W), narrow-strong (N-S), narrow-moderate

TABLE 15
A Matrix of Influence Typology of Explanatory Variables

Scale of Scope	Scale of Intensity		
	Weak	Moderate	Strong
Extensive	E-W	E-M	E-S
Medium	M-W	M-M	M-S
Narrow	N-W	N-M	N-S

(N-M), and narrow-weak (N-W). The matrix of influence typology so developed is shown in Table 15.

Although the model of our influence typology could be applied to map the influence types of all explanatory variable categories for any groupings of policy measures, we applied it only to six policy variable groups. We did not apply this model to other policy groups because the number of policy measures in the other policy groups is too few to make the application of the model meaningful. The six policy groups are all policies in 1962 and 1969, the spending level policies in 1962 and 1969, and the policy changes in the spending levels from 1957 to 1962 and from 1962 to 1969.

The influence types of the eight categories of independent variables for the six policy groups, scaled and mapped, are presented in Figures 1 through 6. Figure 1 shows the 1962 influence typology for all policies. The eight variable categories display five influence types: E-S for economic development and urbanism; M-S for state fiscal system; E-W for apportionment; M-M for political party system, governmental modernism, and political conflict; and N-M for political participation. Economic development and urbanism top both scales of influence and outrank all political-governmental variable categories.

The 1967/1969 influence types for all policies mapped in Figure 2 indicate a general upward shift of political-governmental influences over the 1962 pattern. Reapportionment moved up one scale on intensity, and political conflict and political participation moved up one scale each on scope. On the contrary, urbanism slipped down on both scales of influence.

The comparison of the influence types presented in Figures 1 and 2 permits us to draw the following generalizations:

First, the influence types of political-governmental variables are generally in a fluid state. One half of the variable categories had an upward shift in their influence types from 1962 to 1969.

Second, apportionment gained influence following the so-called reapportionment revolution. It seems evident that reapportionment has in fact significantly realigned the policy orientation of state legislatures as was persistently argued by the reapportionment proponents. This particular finding makes the apprehension expressed by some empirical analysts (see, for example, Dye, 1965; Jacob, 1964) about the future impact of reapportionment largely unwarranted.

Third, political participation and political conflict have gained influence over the two policy periods. These particular changes of the influence types lead us to believe that the movement toward participatory democracy and confrontation politics emerging in the late 1960s has had a democratizing influence in the state policy-making process.

Finally, socioeconomic variables display a loss of influence over time, and particularly in the case of urbanism, as the Sacks-Harris (1964) and Hofferbert (1966) studies discovered. This decline in socioeconomic influence has been counterbalanced by the increase of political-governmental influences. However, it is not clear whether the loss of socioeconomic influence is caused by the increase of political-governmental influence.

Figures 3 and 4 show the influence patterns for the spending level policies only for 1962 and 1969, respectively. The pattern of influence types for the spending level policies are remarkably similar to the influence typology for all policies. However, the typology for the policy changes of spending levels in the two policy periods, as shown in Figures 5 and 6 displays, is distinct. Political-governmental variable categories generally moved up the influence scales, while economic and urbanism variables moved down the influence scales over the two policy periods. The state fiscal system is a less important influence for the policy changes.

This examination of the influence typology of independent variable categories on different policy groups and in different policy periods enables us to make the following generalizations: (1) Some variable categories such as economic development and governmental modernism maintain an influence type which is highly consistent among the different policy groups and between the different policy periods; (2) Some variable categories such as apportionment and political participation maintain an influence type which is consistent among the different policy groups within the same policy period, but distinct between the two different policy periods; and (3) Some variable categories such as political conflict and urbanism show an influence type which varies from one policy group to another and from one policy period to the next.

	Intensity		
SCOPE	WEAK	MODERATE	STRONG
EXTENSIVE	A		G H
MEDIUM		B D F	E
NARROW		C	

NOTE: A= Apportionment
B= Political Party System
C= Political Participation
D= Governmental Modernism
E= State Fiscal System
F= Political Conflict
G= Economic Development
H= Urbanism

Figure 1: All Measures of State Fiscal Policy Outcome and Influence of Pattern of Independent Variables: 1962

	Intensity		
SCOPE	WEAK	MODERATE	STRONG
EXTENSIVE	⧅	A F	G
MEDIUM	⧅	B C D H	E
NARROW	⧅	⧅	⧅

Figure 2: All Measures of State Fiscal Policy Outcomes and Influence Pattern of Independent Variables: 1967-1969

CHAPTER V
CONCLUSIONS

The "theory" that state fiscal policy is primarily determined by state economic conditions seemed too simple and too tautological. Methodological errors, such as overaggregation, and a lack of sensible political and governmental variables served to mislead. Recent challenges to that "theory" have uncovered some of its weaknesses. This analysis can completely modify it.

Our aim was to identify patterns of influence relationships of socioeconomic, and political-governmental variables to the variance of state policy outcomes. Our findings suggest a rather more complex view of

| | Intensity | | |
SCOPE	WEAK	MODERATE	STRONG
EXTENSIVE	A		G H
MEDIUM	B	D F	E
NARROW		C	

Figure 3: Per Capita State Expenditures and Influence Pattern of Independent Variables: 1962

the determinants of state fiscal policy outcomes as well as a middle-ground between the economics versus politics argument.

From the perspective of the individual policies, we derive the following generalizations from our findings:

(1) *Total* state tax and expenditure outcomes are primarily determined by state economic and social circumstances.

(2) State budgetary decisions *by function* vary in the extent to which they are influenced by social and economic as against political and governmental characteristics.
    A. The more the function is shared, either by State aid to local government or by local implementation, the greater the level of political and governmental control over the decision outcomes.

Intensity

SCOPE	WEAK	MODERATE	STRONG
EXTENSIVE		A	G
MEDIUM		B F H	C D E
NARROW			

Figure 4: Per Capita State Expenditures and Influence Pattern of Independent Variables: 1969

    B. The greater the level of political controversy the greater the political and governmental control over decision outcomes.
    C. The more the spending is for person-oriented services, the greater the political and governmental control over decision outcomes.
    D. The more spending is for economy or land-oriented services, the greater the socioeconomic control over the decision outcomes.
(3) Changes in state spending levels for all and individual functions and taxing levels for all and selected sources are primarily determined by politics not economics.

These generalizations seem to us to be not only a better approximation of the complex reality of the policy process, but logically and theoretically

	Intensity		
SCOPE	WEAK	MODERATE	STRONG
EXTENSIVE	A B	H	G
MEDIUM	F	D	
NARROW		C	E

Figure 5: Percent Change in Per Capita State Expenditures and Influence Pattern of Independent Variables: 1957-1962

sensible. The size of the revenue and expenditure pie is closely related to how much is available. We recognize that there is variation between state economic status and the level of tax effort and we suspect that political variables are the best predictors of that variation. But, tax effort, total expenditures, and economic status are sufficiently closely related to support our hypothesis.

Highly controversial issues, such as sales taxes (as against other kinds of taxes)—including their rate and their distribution, welfare (in 1969), highways in 1969, and income redistribution, seem logically to connect to politics and our evidence indicates that they do.

Our analysis shows the increasing politization of fiscal decisions through time. This confirms the Sacks-Harris (1964) and Hofferbert

[51]

Intensity

SCOPE	WEAK	MODERATE	STRONG
EXTENSIVE		A B G	F
MEDIUM		D	C
NARROW	E		H

Figure 6: Percent Change in Per Capita State Expenditures and Influence Pattern of Independent Variables: 1962-1969

(1966) findings that social and economic variables are declining in their influence over fiscal decisions. The politization of relationships between states and their subdivisions seems to increase daily particularly over the issues of state aid, state aid for what (education, highways, etc.) and state aid for whom (city dwellers versus suburbanites). The findings presented here are a strong reflection of these realities.

In a second part, we reorganized our findings and developed a model of influence typology based on two scales of influence—scope and intensity. The model can classify the policy influence of any independent variable categories into nine influence types. The influence types of our eight independent variable categories mapped for six policy groups are diverse and complex ranging from extensive-strong to narrow-weak and from extensive-weak to narrow-strong. However, three broad patterns of influence types are discernible: stable, realigned and stable, and unstable. Economic development (extensive-strong), governmental modernism (medium-moderate), and state fiscal system (medium-strong) are the variable categories with the stable pattern of influence types. The realigned and stable pattern of influence types include apportionment, extensive-weak for the 1962 policies and extensive-moderate for the 1969 policies, and political participation, narrow-moderate for the 1962 policies and mostly medium-strong for the 1969 policies. The unstable pattern of influence types include political conflict, political party system, and urbanism whose influence types shift from policy area to policy area and from one policy period to the other.

We believe this influence typology of the more powerful policy determinants supports the following conclusions:

(1) There is a general permanency in the influence relationships between economic development, governmental modernism, and state fiscal system indicators and a broad range of state fiscal policy decision-making, though their influence types are various.

(2) The influence relationships of political conflict, political party system, and urbanism indicators to state fiscal policy decision-making shift and are unpredictable.

(3) The influence relationships of legislative apportionment and political participation indicators to state fiscal policy decisions are gaining permanency after a period of transition.

NOTES

1. We believe that many earlier analysts have combined state and local governments as one analytical unit not necessarily because state and local governments together act as a decision-making entity, but because of comparability problem across the states. The functions of state and local governments combined maintain a high degree of comparability among the states, but the intra-state assignment of governmental responsibility between state and its localities is irregular. Therefore, when the unit of analysis is constructed without due regard to the unit of decision-making, the combined state-local unit has the advantage of a greater degree of comparability than state-to-state comparison. We solved this comparability problem inherent in the state as a unit of analysis by including fiscal assignment variables in our independent variables. Fiscal assignments measure the state shares of state and local expenditures and taxes and they are labelled state fiscal systems here. For more detailed description of fiscal assignment variables and their implications, see Campbell and Sacks (1967) and Cho (1967).

2. State direct spending for public welfare represents only a part of state contribution to welfare effort in 15 states where public welfare is directly administered by local governments which disburse state provided funds. Nationally, local contribution to public welfare funds is rather moderate, accounting for only 12 percent of state and local combined expenditures for the function. Therefore, state and local combined expenditures are a more appropriate indicator of the full welfare effort by the states.

3. This variable is taken from Fry and Winters (1970).

4. The 1967 version of this variable is not directly comparable to Fry and Winters' 1961 measure; we took "net cash income" in 1967 to define income classes from *Sales Management,* and the 1965 Tax Foundation classification of the incidence of tax burden and expenditure benefit by income classes on a nation-wide basis is applied to individual states for the computation of state-by-state incidence of tax burden and expenditure benefit and the ratio of the two. Thus, the procedures used for the computation follows those used by Fry and Winters for their 1961 variable.

5. Legislative apportionment includes six measures of malapportionment, ten measures of reapportionment, and six measures of apportionment change from malapportionment to reapportionment. Because of the central concern of the parental study for which these data are collected, the apportionment measures are much more elaborate than other variables included.

6. The measure of state-local conflict is based on the variables of state-local political conflict that Elazar listed in his book (1966). An equal weight is arbitrarily assigned to each of the seven conflict variables for the computation of conflict score for each state. If a state had all seven variables of state-local conflict, a score of 100 was given to that state, while a score of 71.4 was given to a state when that state had five conflict variables out of the possible maximum of seven, for example.

7. Relating a set of common independent variables to several different dependent variables, each in a separate equation, is a common and long practiced analytical technique. See, for example, Fabricant (1952) and Dye (1966).

8. Our classification of policy categories is based on two criteria: policy decision contexts such as how much to spend and how to distribute the spending among various purposes; and, policy substance such as taxation, expenditure, and mix of taxation and expenditures (redistribution). However, the criterion for our classification is rather broadly defined. Thus, the policy measures included in each policy group are not always completely homogeneous.

9. This technique was also used by Sharkansky (1970). However, this technique does not quite solve the problem of multi-collinearity, but our check on the inter-correlations among the variables so selected indicated that multi-collinearity is not a serious problem in our case.

10. An alternative to this selection method of independent variables can be factor analysis which can be used to collapse the independent variables into a relatively small number of factors and a factor score can be computed for each of the factors. We rejected this approach because factor score is so high a level of abstraction of the real value of any of the variables actually used that its relationships to dependent variables present an insurmountable problem of sensible interpretation.

11. When the apportionment measure ranks seventh in its explanatory power, there is a possibility that there might be some other variables which are more powerful than the apportionment measure but not included in the equation. Even in that case, the explanatory power of the six other variables in the equation is not

distorted because the explanatory power added by the apportionment measure is marginal. Therefore, we are not convinced that we will obtain a different result from the one we have already obtained here by re-running regressions for each of the 94 policy variables out of the combined pool of apportionment measures and other independent variables.

12. The information shown in the third column of the first line of Table 1 should be read as follows: the number 4 represents the fourth variable of apportionment measures (A) as shown in the independent variable list (that is, the David-Eisenburg Smallest County Index) and the figure in the parenthesis (.017) indicates the increment in the R^2 contributed by the David-Eisenberg Smallest County Index.

13. The tables presented in the text are summarized from the detailed information showing the relationship of each of the explanatory variables to the policy measure. For example, the detailed information from which the summary information for the first equation in Table 1 (per capita total general expenditures) is extracted from the following table.

Per Capita Total General Expenditure, 1962

Relations with	r	Regression Coefficient	$\triangle R^2$
Political-Governmental vs. ($\Sigma \triangle R^2$)			.351
Expenditure Assignment, 1962	.512	502.644	.262
Civil Service Coverage	.176	67.656	.072
David-Eisenberg Small Co. Index, 1962	-.040	.496	.017
Socio-Economic Variables ($\Sigma \triangle R^2$)			.471
Education, 1960	.385	13.944	.332
Change in Urbanization, 50-60	.380	.420	.041
PCI. 1962	.246	.064	.032
Industrialization, 1960	.050	-2.826	.067
R^2			.822
R			.907

14. In our view, the tendency that greater professional capability of legislatures is converted into the means of stengthening the watchdog role of public spending seems to be reinforced by the surging taxpayers' rebellion in recent years.

15. Dye (1969) reasons that political support for sales taxes is easier to mobilize than other taxes, particularly when taxes on such legal vices as cigarettes and alcoholic beverages are brought to political consideration.

16. The 1962 nationwide average of state expenditures in metropolitan and nonmetropolitan areas for total aid (per capita), school aid (per pupil), highways (per capita), and public welfare (per capita) shows consistent disparity in favor of nonmetropolitan areas. The disparity ranged from the high of 274 percent in direct highway spending to the low of 24 percent in school aid.

17. The level of variance explained by Fry and Winters was considerably higher than ours. This difference may be caused by the number of explanatory variables included in the regression equations. They used 18 variables compared with seven in our study.

REFERENCES

Advisory Commission of Intergovernmental Relations (1966) Tax Overlapping in the United States, A Supplement to Report M-23. Washington, D.C.: Government Printing Office.
CAMPBELL, A. K. and S. SACKS (1967) Metropolitan America: Fiscal Patterns and Governmental Systems. New York: Free Press.
CHO, Y. H. (1967) "The effect of local governmental systems on local policy outcomes in the United States." Public Admin. Rev. 27 (March).
--- and H. G. FREDERICKSON (1973) "Measuring the effects of reapportionment in the American states." A Report to the National Municipal League.
CNUDDE, C. F. and D. J. McCRONE (1969) "Party competition and welfare policies in the American states." Amer. Pol. Sci. Rev. 63 (September).
DAWSON, R. E. and J. A. ROBINSON (1963) "Interstate competition, economic variables and welfare policies in the American states." J. of Politics 25.
DYE, T. R. (1969a) "Income inequality and American state politics." Amer. Pol. Sci. Rev. 63 (March).
--- (1969b) Politics in States and Communities. Englewood Cliffs, N.J.: Prentice-Hall.
--- (1966) Politics, Economics and the Public: Policy Outcomes in the American States. Chicago: Rand McNally.
--- (1965) "Malapportionment and public policy in the states." J. of Politics 27 (August).
ELAZAR, D. (1966) American Federalism: A View From the States. New York: Thomas Y. Crowell.
FABRICANT, S. (1952) The Trend of Government Activity in the United States Since 1900. New York: National Bureau of Economic Research.
FISHER, G. W. (1964) "Interstate variation in state and local government expenditures." Nat'l Tax J. 17.
FRY, B. and R. WINTERS (1970) "The politics of redistribution." Amer. Pol. Sci. Rev. 64 (December).
HOFFERBERT, R. I. (1966) "Ecological development and policy change." Midwest J. of Pol. Sci. 10.
JACOB, H. (1964) "The consequences of malapportionment: a note of caution." Social Forces 43 (December).
KEY, V. O. (1949) Southern Politics. New York: Vintage.
PULSIPHER, A. and J. WEATHERBY (1968) "Malapportionment, party competition, and the functional distribution of government expenditures." Amer. Pol. Sci. Rev. 62 (December).
SACKS, S. and R. HARRIS (1964) "The determinants of state and local government expenditures and intergovernmental flows of funds." Nat'l. Tax J. 17 (March).
SHARKANSKY, I. (1970) Regionalism in American Politics. Indianapolis: Bobbs-Merrill.
--- (1968) "Agency requests, gubernatorial support and budget success in state legislatures." Amer. Pol. Sci. Rev. 62 (December).
U.S. Bureau of the Census (1964) Compendium of Government Finances. Washington, D.C.: Government Printing Office.

Augsburg College
George Sverdrup Library
Minneapolis, Minnesota 55404

A Better Way of Getting New Information

Research, survey and policy studies that say what needs to be said—no more, no less.

The Sage Papers Program

Five regularly-issued original paperback series that bring, at an unusually low cost, the timely writings and findings of the international scholarly community. Since the material is updated on a continuing basis, each series rapidly becomes a unique repository of vital information.

Authoritative, and frequently seminal, works that NEED to be available

- To scholars and practitioners
- In university and institutional libraries
- In departmental collections
- For classroom adoption

Sage Professional Papers

COMPARATIVE POLITICS SERIES
INTERNATIONAL STUDIES SERIES
ADMINISTRATIVE AND POLICY STUDIES SERIES
AMERICAN POLITICS SERIES

Sage Policy Papers

THE WASHINGTON PAPERS

SAGE PUBLICATIONS
The Publishers of Professional Social Science
Beverly Hills • London

Sage Professional Papers in Comparative Politics

Editors: **Harry Eckstein,** *Princeton University,* **Ted Robert Gurr,** *Northwestern University,* and **Aristide R. Zolberg,** *University of Chicago.*

VOLUME 1 (1970)

- 01-001 **J.Z. Namenwirth & H. D. Lasswell,** The changing language of American values: a computer study of selected party platforms $2.50/£1.05
- 01-002 **K. Janda,** A conceptual framework for the comparative analysis of political parties $1.90/£.80
- 01-003 **K. Thompson,** Cross-national voting behavior research $1.50/£.60
- 01-004 **W. B. Quandt,** The comparative study of political elites $2.00/£.85
- 01-005 **M. C. Hudson,** Conditions of political violence and instability $1.90/£.80
- 01-006 **E. Ozbudun,** Party cohesion in western democracies $3.00/£1.30
- 01-007 **J. R. Nellis,** A model of developmental ideology in Africa $1.40/£.55
- 01-008 **A. Kornberg, et al.,** Semi-careers in political organizations $1.40/£.55
- 01-009 **F. I. Greenstein & S. Tarrow,** Political orientations of children $2.90/£1.25
- 01-010 **F. W. Riggs,** Administrative reform and political responsiveness: a theory of dynamic balance $1.50/£.60
- 01-011 **R. H. Donaldson & D. J. Waller,** Stasis and change in revolutionary elites: a comparative analysis of the 1956 Central Party Committees in China and the USSR $1.90/£.80
- 01-012 **R. A. Pride,** Origins of democracy: a cross-national study of mobilization, party systems and democratic stability $2.90/£1.25

VOLUME II (1971)

- 01-013 **S. Verba, et al.,** The modes of democratic participation $2.80/£1.20
- 01-014 **W. R. Schonfeld,** Youth and authority in France $2.80/£1.20
- 01-015 **S. J. Bodenheimer,** The ideology of developmentalism $2.40/£1.00
- 01-016 **L. Sigelman,** Modernization and the political system $2.50/£1.05
- 01-017 **H. Eckstein,** The evaluation of political performance: problems and dimensions $2.90/£1.25
- 01-018 **T. Gurr & M. McLelland,** Political performance: a twelve nation study $2.90/£1.25
- 01-019 **R. F. Moy,** A computer simulation of democratic political development $2.70/£1.15
- 01-020 **T. Nardin,** Violence and the state $2.70/£1.15
- 01-021 **W. Ilchman,** Comparative public administration and "conventional wisdom" $2.40/£1.00
- 01-022 **G. Bertsch,** Nation-building in Yugoslavia $2.25/£.95
- 01-023 **R. J. Willey,** Democracy in West German trade unions $2.40/£1.00
- 01-024 **R. Rogowski & L. Wasserspring,** Does political development exist? Corporatism in old and new societies $2.40/£1.00

VOLUME III (1972)

- 01-025 **W. T. Daly,** The revolutionary $2.10/£.90
- 01-026 **C. Stone,** Stratification and political change in Trinidad and Jamaica $2.10/£.90
- 01-027 **Z. Y. Gitelman,** The diffusion of political innovation: from Eastern Europe to the Soviet Union $2.50/£1.05
- 01-028 **D. P. Conradt,** The West German party system $2.40/£1.00
- 01-029 **J. R. Scarritt,** Political development and culture change theory [Africa] $2.50/£1.05
- 01-030 **M. D. Hayes,** Policy outputs in the Brazilian states $2.25/£.95
- 01-031 **B. Stallings,** Economic dependency in Africa and Latin America $2.50/£1.05
- 01-032 **J. T. Campos & J. F. McCamant,** Cleavage shift in Colombia: analysis of the 1970 elections $2.90/£1.25
- 01-033 **G. Field & J. Higley,** Elites in developed societies [Norway] $2.25/£.95
- 01-034 **J. S. Szyliowicz,** A political analysis of student activism [Turkey] $2.80/£1.20
- 01-035 **E. C. Hargrove,** Professional roles in society and government [England] $2.90/£1.25
- 01-036 **A. J. Sofranko & R. J. Bealer,** Unbalanced modernization and domestic instability $2.90/£1.25

VOLUME IV (1973)

- 01-037 **W. A. Cornelius,** Political learning among the migrant poor $2.90/£1.25
- 01-038 **J. W. White,** Political implications of cityward migration [Japan] $2.50/£1.05
- 01-039 **R. B. Stauffer,** Nation-building in a global economy: the role of the multi-national corporation $2.25/£.95
- 01-040 **A. Martin,** The politics of economic policy in the U.S. $2.50/£1.05

Forthcoming, summer/fall 1973

- 01-041 **M. B. Welfling,** Political Institutionalization [African party systems] $2.70*/£1.15
- 01-042 **B. Ames,** Rhetoric and reality in a militarized regime [Brazil] $2.40*/£1.00
- 01-043 **E. C. Browne,** Coalition theories $2.90*/£1.25
- 01-044 **M. Barrera,** Information and ideology: a study of Arturo Frondizi $2.40*/£1.00

*denotes tentative price

Papers 01-045 through 01-048 to be announced.

Sage Professional Papers in

Editor: Vincent Davis *and* Mauri...

VOLUME I (1972)

02-001	E. E. Azar, et al., Inter... events interaction anal... $2.80/£1.20
02-002	J. H. Sigler, et al., App... events data analysis
02-003	J. C. Burt, Decision ne... the world population ... $2.25/£.95
02-004	J. A. Caporaso, Functi... regional integration
02-005	E. R. Wittkopf, Weste... aid allocations $2.5...
02-006	T. L. Brewer, Foreign ... tions: American elite ... variations in threat, ti... surprise $2.50/£1.0...
02-007	W. F. Weiker, Decentr... ernment in moderniz[i]... [Turkish provinces]
02-008	F. A. Beer, The politi... of alliances: benefits, ... institutions in NATO
02-009	C. Mesa-Lago. The lab... employment, unempl... underemployment in ... 1970 $2.70/£1.15
02-010	P. M. Burgess & R. W... cators of internationa... an assessment of ever... research $3.00/£1....
02-011	W. Minter, Imperial ... external dependency ... $2.70/£1.15

Sage Professional Papers

Administra...

Editor: H. George Fredericks...

VOLUME I (1973)

03-001	E. Ostrom, W. Bau... R. Parks, G. Whita... organization and t... police services $
03-002	R. S. Ahlbrandt, J... protection services
03-003	D. O. Porter with ... T. W. Porter. The ... ing federal aid [Io... $3.00/£1.30
03-004	J. P. Viteritti, Pol... pluralism in New ... $2.70/£1.15

The 1973 summer/fall paper...

03-005	R. L. Schott, Pro... service: character... tion of engineer f...

ORDER FORM

name _____

institution _____

address _____

city/state/zip _____

Please enter subscription(s) to:

☐ Prof. Pprs. in Administrative & Policy Studies
☐ Prof. Pprs. in Comparative Politics
☐ Prof. Pprs. in American Politics
☐ Prof. Pprs. in International Studies
☐ The Washington Papers

Please send the individual papers whose numbers I have listed below:

_____
_____
_____

☐ Please invoice (INSTITUTIONS ONLY) quoting P.O. # _____ (shipping and handling additional on non-subscription orders)

☐ Payment enclosed (Sage pays shipping charges)

INSTITUTIONAL ORDERS FOR LESS THAN $10.00 AND *ALL* PERSONAL ORDERS *MUST BE PREPAID*. (California residents: please add 6% sales tax on non-subscription orders.)

MAIL TO:

SAGE Publications, Inc. / P.O. Box 5024 Beverly Hills, California 90210

orders from the U.K., Europe, the Middle East and Africa should be sent to Sage Publications, Ltd, 44 Hatton Garden, London EC1N 8ER

A Sage Policy Papers Series

The Washington Papers

... intended to meet the need for authoritative, yet prompt, public appraisal of the major changes in world affairs. Commissioned and written under the auspices of the Center for Strategic and International Studies (CSIS), Georgetown University, Washington, D.C. and published for CSIS by SAGE Publications; Beverly Hills/London.

Series Editor: Walter Laqueur, *Director of the Institute of Contemporary History (London) and Chairman, CSIS, Research Council, Georgetown University*

Price Information: Individual papers in the series are available at $2.50/£1.00 each.

Save on subscriptions: Individuals and institutions can realize substantial savings by entering a subscription order (commencing with Volume I) at the prices given below.

	1 year†	2 year	3 year
Institutional	$20/£8.50	$39/£16.50	$57/£24.00
Individual	$12/£5.40	$23/£10.40	$33/£15.40

†See note on frequency below

Frequency: Volume 1 (September 1972 through December 1973) will include 12 papers published over a 16-month period. Beginning with Volume II (1974), Ten papers will be published each calendar year—and mailed to subscribers in groups of 3 or 4 throughout the year.

Specially commissioned to bring you authoritative evaluations of major events affecting (and affected by) current developments in U.S. foreign policy and world affairs. THE WASHINGTON PAPERS offer timely, provocative, in-depth analyses by leading authorities—who also suggest likely future developments and analyze the policy implications of recent trends.

VOLUME I (1972-73)

$2.50 each /£1.00

- WP-1 R. M. Burrell, The Persian Gulf
- WP-2 R. Scalapino, American-Japanese relations in a changing era
- WP-3 E. Luttwak, The strategic balance, 1972
- WP-4 C. Issawi, Oil, the Middle East and the world
- WP-5 W. Laqueur, Neo-isolationism and the world of the seventies
- WP-6 W. E. Griffith, Peking, Moscow and beyond
- WP-7 R. M. Burrell & A. J. Cottrell, Politics, oil and the western Mediterranean
- WP-8 P. Hassner, Europe in the age of negotiation
- WP-9 W. Joshua & W. F. Hahn, Nuclear politics: America, France and Britain

Forthcoming
- WP-10 T. A. Sumberg, Foreign aid as a moral obligation?
- WP-11 H. Block, Trade with the Soviet Union
- WP-12 R. Moss, Hijacking

Sage Professional Papers in **American Politics**

Editor: Randall B. Ripley, *Ohio State University.*

VOLUME I (1973)

- 04-001 S. S. Nagel, Comparing elected and appointed judicial systems $2.25/£1.95
- 04-002 J. Dennis, Political socialization research: a bibliography $2.40/£1.00
- 04-003 H. B. Asher, Freshman represer atives and the learning of votin cues $2.50/£1.05
- 04-004 J. Fishel, Representation and responsiveness in Congress: "th class of eighty-nine," 1965-197 $2.70/£1.15

Papers 04-005 through 04-012 to be announce

MAIL TO
SAGE Publications / P.O. Box 5024 / Beverly Hills, Calif. 90210
orders from the U.K., Europe, the Middle East and Africa
should be sent to 44 Hatton Garden, London EC1N 8ER